# The Queen

## The Archetype of Leadership

# Brian Dale

## Illustrated by Lily Loy

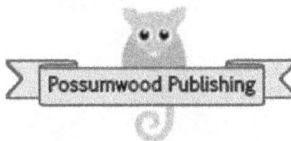

Possumwood Publishing

Possumwood Publishing
5 Possumwood Place, Mullumbimby, NSW 2482
Australia
possumwoodpublishing@gmail.com


First published in 2017

Dale, Brian Richard
The Queen
Archetypes
Personality traits
Psychology
Spirituality

Illustrations by Lily Loy
Cover illustration and design by Lily Loy
Editing and typesetting by Jan Dale

Printed by CreateSpace, An Amazon.com Company
Published by Possumwood Publishing

# Dedication

This book is dedicated to my dear sister, Jan Dale.

She is the epitome of the Queen archetype, responsible, independent, and successful and with an overwhelming sense of justice and duty.

# Table of Contents

# The Queen

How to rule with authority and benevolence; achieve your ambitions and goals; and still be loved and admired by your subjects and all those who surround you.

### Yes! You are the Queen.

You know that it is true. Why else would you take charge and be in control. Why are you the most important person in your group? Why are you the only one capable of doing everything as it should be done and without errors? Why are you the only one that you can trust in?

### It is because you have the Queen archetype.

Your family and friends recognize that part of your personality. They know that you are a Queen. They understand that you will take charge in difficult situations. They are looking for leadership and you can provide it.

### This happens because you have the archetypal energy of the Queen.

All your subjects understand that it is a fact of life for you and for them. They may call you "bossy" or "hard to get along with". That is because you are in charge. You have responsibilities and duties. You cannot please all of the people all of the time and you understand that.

### The archetypal energy of the Queen is used to maintain your rule and your realm.

All the people you deal with observe this quality and respect your position and energy. When you are working to preserve, maintain or improve your realm, others are there to offer their service or advice. This will usually come at a cost. Others realize that you have control of the decision making and the purse strings.

### The archetypal energy of the Queen is a strong energy that has a powerful influence.

2

# Recognition of the Queen Archetype

*So how do we deal with the energy and authority of the Queen?*

Individuals with the Queen archetype usually recognize their position, their power and the archetypal energy. They may have little or no understanding of archetypes. They may or may not call themselves a Queen. However, they will recognize the energy and responsibility.

If there has been some amazing misunderstanding; a life of consistent self-deprecation; or an over-powering relationship there may be confusion and denial. So let us clear up any misunderstandings. Let us begin to elevate your position and your power. Let us deal with relationships with clarity and action.

**You are a Queen.**

**Recognize the Queen archetype.**

**Use the archetypal energy for personal and group achievement.**

So how do we deal with the Queen and recognize the accompanying archetypal energy?

Queens:

❖ have a realm
❖ take control and authority of the issues that need dealing with
❖ have an overwhelming need to do everything themselves. If there is delegation it is to a trusted advisor or associates and scrutiny is observed
❖ are in charge of the spending and the money. If there is spending it goes to advancing the realm or to the upholding of the royal tradition
❖ are good at saving and retaining sufficient funds to ward off the threat of bankruptcy
❖ pay attention to their appearance and protocol especially when in their court or the public eye

❖ are reluctant to encroach on another's kingdom or realm unless they are confident they can win any ensuing battle

❖ often set themselves apart or consider themselves above ordinary people especially if these people are below the Queen in rank or are her subjects.

Have you got the picture?

**Have you recognized the Queen archetype as part of your personality?**

**Do you understand that you use the Queen archetypal energy in various situations and on a daily basis?**

Good! So let us proceed.

# The Queen Archetype

How to:

- ❖ rule with authority and benevolence

- ❖ achieve your ambitions and goals and

- ❖ still be loved and admired by your subjects and all those who surround you.

# Respect

The position of Queen is powerful. There will be many people and events effected or changed by the behaviour and decision-making of the Queen. Positions of power demand responsibility. Some Queens will rise to the challenge and use this power wisely and for the benefit of all. Others will not. They will seek personal glorification and misuse their power for their own comfort and to the disadvantage of others.

The Queen can be a benevolent Queen respected by those in her realm and admired by outsiders.

She can also be a dictator; her reign dependent on self-serving bullies and paid henchmen; her guru status; by the intimidation of her power; by fear; by coercion.

## What kind of Queen are you?

The first step to being a benevolent and respected Queen is to have respect. There is respect for you as an individual. This begins with you.

- ❖ What is your self-image? Is it positive?
- ❖ Do you like yourself?
- ❖ Are you pleased with who you are?
- ❖ Are you comfortable with your role as Queen?

## Respect yourself.

Consider your personal habits, your health, your diet, your exercise regime, how you dress, what you say and think to yourself, etc. If there are changes to be made begin now. Changing personal habits that are detrimental to your well-being is never easy. However, individuals with the Queen archetype have incredible resilience and determination. Success can be yours when you make a decision and take one step at a time. Busy people often have the Queen archetype. There is always an excuse to rush meals, forgo exercise, etc. Change the priorities and make time. Change begins with you respecting who you are and how you are best equipped to rule.

## Respect others.

Accepting other individuals for who they are is showing respect for them. You do not have to like them. However you may have to deal with them or work with them. Treat them with respect and personalities should not enter into this relationship. If you are in the position of power then use your authority but give recognition to the contribution of others.

The archetypal energy and personality traits of the Queen will automatically dictate that you be placed above others. The Queen is at the top of the hierarchy. Respect that position of responsibility and respect the opinions of others in the hierarchy that are willing to accept the status quo. Queens do not have a realm unless there are others to support her position and accept theirs.

## Respect other realms.

Kings and Queens create a battlefield when they encroach on the others territory. Two of my favourite relatives have a King and a Queen archetype. They have had previous relationships and their pattern of behaviour towards home duties has been well-established. He likes to cook. She sees cooking the family meal as part of her duties. Hence the battlefield is in the kitchen. Their disagreements are nothing major and will not harm their relationship. I use it as a simple example.

There have always been and still are major disagreements between individuals with the King and Queen archetypes that lead countries or tribes. This disagreement often leads to destruction and harm to both realm and the subjects within those realms. Look at the leadership battles within political parties. Observe the rivalry between businesses competing for the same market share.

Understand your relationship within your work environment. Are you one of two Queens competing for the same position, the same work space, the same reward or recognition, etc? Is there a clarification of duties and responsibilities or is there a continual battle over territory or striving to prove one's worth when compared with the other.

I recall a young student in a continual battle with a teacher. This child had a strong Queen archetype and she was constantly fighting with the teacher for authority and territory. The solution was simple. Give this child responsibility and duties within the classroom that are her domain. At the same time remind this child that the teacher is responsible for the students and the rest of the classroom management. This is showing respect. The child is being shown respect for her ability to be in charge and be responsible. At the same time there is the expectation that she shows equal respect towards the teacher and her duties.

**Respect is the cornerstone to a healthy and positive reign as Queen.**

**Never underestimate the power of respect.**

# Understand your Realm

All Queens will seek opportunities to rule or to establish a realm. You may be the power within your family. Here the home, family routine and family members are your realm and your subjects. Your work may find you in a business or corporation. You may be in charge of a department. Individuals with the Queen archetype will be drawn to management positions. Here lays the responsibility to improve the productivity of your realm and the company's bottom line. Your success may prove to be a stepping stone to take charge of the whole company. Other individuals start their own business. This is a natural path as the Queen will always be in control and working long hours to do what has to be done is not foreign to the Queen archetypal energy. Queens will often go into teaching. Their classrooms or curriculum departments become suitable realms. The Queen energy and personality is also found in clubs and service organizations. Presidents and chairpersons of these organizations are the ideal positions for the Queen.

Once you understand that you are a Queen you need to define your realm and your position of power.

What is the extent of your realm? What are the limitations of your control and power? Are you part of a bigger realm? Are you answerable to another power further up the hierarchy? Who are your subjects? What are their responsibilities? Who are your advisors? Are these the best people for the job? Are your realm and your subjects as productive as they can be? Is consolidation or expansion needed?

This brings us nicely into the next key to your success; planning.

# Plan

Once you have established an idea or have become involved in a business or organization you can begin to plan your success and its development. One of the keys to success is planning. If you, as the Queen, desire longevity and success in your venture you are well served to plan.

The length and nature of the planning is your decision. Planning is an individual choice. The intensity of the planning process will depend on your personality and your other archetypes. If you are an intuitive person you will allow your Saboteur archetype or "gut feeling" to take control. This type of planning is done quickly and is open to a large degree of flexibility and adaptation. If you use your Philosopher or Seeker archetype your planning will be extensive and written with all the many possibilities, pros and cons.

Remember planning is an individual choice. However, the most important step is to put your thoughts and plans into action.

## Action! Action! Action!

Never allow the Philosopher or Seeker archetype to bamboozle you with all the possibilities.

> *"I need to consider all the options."*
>
> *"I have to assess the situation."*
>
> *"I need more information."*

These are the favourite expressions of the Philosopher and the Seeker and they rotate round and round in an individual's thought pattern and cause a state of paralysis. Choose an action plan and go for it.

Never allow the Coward archetype to dissuade or discourage you.

> *"What will people think?"*
>
> *"I haven't got time."*
>
> *"I will begin tomorrow."*

These are favourite expressions of the Coward and they are designed to denigrate and delay.

The positive side of the Coward is the Hero. So grab that "nervous nelly" of your Coward archetype, say

*"This is what we are doing. You are going to help me.*

*There is to be no argument and no discussion. You have made a decision and that is the end of the matter.*

Choose an action plan and go for it.

If things do not go according to plan then change your plan. Never be discouraged or disheartened by the "I made a mistake" philosophy. Everything we do is learning. Mistakes are a means to learning. Learn from what you have done and make your next action more effective.

**Once your ideas are placed in to action, monitor their progress.**

The planning never stops. Continually assess your plans. Keep looking forward to what else can you do and what else you can achieve. Keep looking sideways to see if you can do things more effectively.

Beware of becoming insular and dogmatic. The world is constantly changing; technology is rapidly changing. Take on board those new ideas that can strengthen you personally or corporately.

Keep in mind that many things move in cycles. The development of the Queen and her domain will progress at varying rates. Enjoy the good times and work through the more challenging times. If your empire collapses begin work on another. If one job opportunity closes seek another. If a relationship fails develop another.

**Remember! You are the Queen.**

# Affirm

Affirmations are powerful tools. Affirmations do not need to be complicated or comprehensive.

There was a period; it may still exist, where the individual had to go to great lengths to affirm the changes that they desired. Journals, meditations, positive pictures placed on fridges, etc. Yes! They are valuable.

However, all of this action can be negated by an individual's self talk and thought patterns. When credit is due, give yourself credit.

> *"That was well done."*
>
> *"I have done a good job there."*
>
> *"This is fantastic."*
>
> *"This is working well."*

All of these are affirmations. They may only be a thought or a sentence spoken quietly; yet they are powerful and meaningful affirmations.

## *Remember:*

**Affirmations are to be positive and in the present.**

Words and phrases such as

> *"When"*   *"I will"*   *"if only"*   *"next week"*   *"I must"*

These and similar expressions do not deliver and will not effect change.

How many people keep saying?

> *"When I win the lotto I will . . . .?"*

Apart from the mathematical odds stacked against them they are continually affirming action or change sometime in the future, not the present.

Life is lived in the present. Use words and phrases such as

> *"I am"*      *"now"*      *"I have"*      *"always"*

These are statements are positive and in the present. These affirmations deliver results.

# Delegate

Authority and knowledge are vital aspects of the Queen archetypal energy. As a Queen you need to be in charge. You need to know what goes on in your realm. This requires a strong work ethic and a consistent work pattern. These are the hallmarks of a successful Queen. As the Queen you are prepared to make sacrifices. You are prepared to take on responsibilities. You are prepared to work long and hard to achieve success. You know and understand that you are the best person to get the job done.

So now we come to the one of the most difficult decisions you as Queen will have to make. That decision is one of delegation. If you are in charge of your own business or your realm is small enough for a total "hands-on" management approach you may be able to do everything yourself. However, if your realm expands or if you are part of a bigger organization you will not be able to do everything and you will have to delegate. This is never an easy decision for the Queen. Letting go is not easy. Look at Queen Elizabeth II.

Nevertheless there comes a time when delegation is essential. What to do? The answer comes back to trust. The Queen needs to trust in those individuals who take over key responsibilities that, because of time or workload, the Queen can no longer manage.

Find associates that have your confidence and trust.

History is a remarkably educative tool. Britain's Queen Elizabeth I and Queen Victoria are perfect examples of women taking charge of the nation at a very young age. Both had limited experience in politics or worldly affairs. Yet both had long and successful reigns overseeing Britain flourish as a nation both internally and externally.

Certainly they both called upon their Queen archetypal energy to rule, dominate and influence. However, they also used their judgment to surround them with trusted advisors. Elizabeth relied upon William Cecil and Francis Drake. Queen Victoria relied initially upon Lord Melbourne and later her husband Albert.

**Find two trusted advisors and associates.**

Working with two trusted advisors gives you, the Queen, the power and ability to monitor your realm and expand your domain. Two advisors form a triangle with the Queen perched on the apex. The triangle, of course, is the strongest shape and from that formation the hierarchy is able to expand downwards and outwards.

Find your trusted associates and delegate. This gives you the power to consolidate and expand your realm.

# Pride

As a Queen you should always take pride in your achievements and your success. Pride in your accomplishments gives you the momentum for further success. It is a great motivational tool.

**Use pride wisely and with discretion.**

Pride should never be used for bragging; for showing off; for lauding your success over your opponents.

At a personal level, pride should be an internal and personal emotion.

When used within the organization use it as a low-key motivator. Excessive pride and hype works well in the short term. However, when the enthusiasm wears off; when more challenging times arrive; false promises, exaggerated expectations and emotional highs are more likely to create disillusionment and bitterness. Pride and respect work well together. They provide a great balance and create an atmosphere where the individuals within the realm feel comfortable in doing their best and content with the rewards of their labour.

As a Queen you need to understand that although you are motivated and prepared for hard work your subjects may not share those same emotions. Show them respect and demonstrate pride in your behaviour. This is an excellent way to encourage loyalty, a strong work ethic and to share in a win-win situation for all concerned.

When used externally, pride should be used to enhance reputation. Your reputation as an individual or an organization is vital to your success and longevity. The Queen and her realm will not survive without a reliable reputation. A solid reputation attracts both customers and workers. Pride, used as a low-key component, enhances your reputation. It shows people outside your organization that you care not only for those in your realm but also for the impact you make on those outside your realm.

**Pride is a great friend; never make it your enemy.**

# Longevity

Understand that the Queen archetype is with you all of your life. You do not lose or gain any archetypes. Your personal archetypes are you. They are your personality. They determine how you react and behave in the different situations that confront you. With this in mind, understand that you will always be the personality that creates a realm and takes control.

Life is full of experiences. You, as a Queen, are not guaranteed permanent reign in any one particular situation, employment or relationship. You may be able to build a business that lasts you a lifetime; work for a company that spans your working life; have a career in teaching; be in a relationship that stands the test of time. If that is your choice and it works for you; good luck! You are brilliant. Enjoy the journey and rejoice in your achievement. However, for many of you your reign will be shorter in duration. Your possible challenge may be to let go. Once your reign is over and your realm dissipates it is time to move on to the next challenge. Never dwell in past glories or wallow in the 'failure' syndrome. Accept the experience; learn from it and move on to the next challenge.

The concept of retirement is a challenge to the Queen. From a psychological and spiritual point of view, for the Queen, there is no such thing as retirement. As the Queen ages or her circumstances change, she may find her capacity to continue in her employment or business diminish. Circumstances of retirement, illness or poverty may be a cause of frustration and restlessness. However, it is important for the individual to come to terms with the limitations placed upon them and their capacity to serve and rule. They will still find some outlet for the Queen energy, even though this may be an activity or domain of small significance when compared with previous accomplishments. Yet this is the way of the physical world and the cycle of our earthly existence. The Queen's attitude may have to change to the acceptance a lesser role.

**Remember you are a Queen for life.**

# Money and the Royal Coffers

As Queen and head of the realm you are in charge of the finances. You may not be involved in the book keeping but you certainly are in charge of the spending. If that is not your responsibility there may be a need to negotiate or you may be subject to a ruler in a loftier hierarchical position.

Queens are very good at saving and managing resources. They are also good with spending sprees. The two are not diametrically opposed. The usual nature of the Queen archetype is to save. When there is sufficient money in the kitty much of that will be spent. The spending will not be wasted. It will go towards making the realm a better or more efficient place or upholding the traditions and protocols.

Your task as the Queen is to make sure that overspending does not occur. A bankrupt realm will not survive or will be ineffective in its purpose. You need to keep a wary eye on the spendthrifts. Individuals with the archetypes of Addict, Angel, Damsel, Entrepreneur, Fairy, Fool, Goddess, Lover, Prince, Princess, Rebel and Thief will spend, sometimes with reckless abandon. They may bring positive benefits to your relationship or your realm but they need to be quarantined from having access to the royal coffers.

Keep in mind that money and resources have a dual purpose. They exist to keep the realm in existence. Therefore, it is wise to keep some resources for a 'rainy day' or for an emergency. They also exist to consolidate and expand the realm. Hence; spend wisely.

# Service

Finally, but most importantly, always keep in mind that the Queen's role is one of service. Your role as Queen is to lead. You are in charge and leadership is vital. You are also the protector of your realm and all that is found there. Your duties are many and varied and your responsibilities are never to be forgotten.

**You are a servant of the realm you have created.**

It is easy to be lost in the power; in the work ethic; in the success; in the admiration and adulation. Throughout the history of human endeavour there have always been leaders who thrive on the power, the control and the glorification. This is the negative archetypal energy of leadership archetypes.

Some individuals move into positions of power and control with the use of this negative energy. When they reach the top, this negative energy is empowered and gratified. These are the dictators, the autocrats, the megalomaniacs, the control freaks and the bullies. They may lead a nation or they may just be the head of a household or local club. The archetypal energy is negative. Their first impulse and duty is to serve their own ego. Their second impulse and duty is to reward their loyal enforcers and sycophants. Their third impulse is to use and take advantage of their subjects. Their ego and their paid band of adoring followers create the world of illusion. This illusion creates and maintains the false belief that these rulers serve the people. It creates and maintains the false belief that they are loved and adored. This world of illusion is difficult to maintain. The negative energy of corruption, coercion and fear eventually breaks down and these rulers are seen for what they truly are. They are the servant of their own ego but not the servant of their people.

**Always keep in mind what you are striving for:**

- ❖ **to rule with authority and benevolence**
- ❖ **to achieve your ambitions and goals**
- ❖ **to be loved and admired by your subjects and all those who surround you.**

18

The positive energy of the Queen archetype is just as powerful as the negative energy of the Queen archetype. However, the true benefit of the positive Queen archetypal energy is the creation, encouragement and maintenance of all the other archetypal energies that are used to build and sustain her realm.

As you build your realm; develop your relationships; assist others within your sphere of influence. There is an abundance of positive energy flowing from your subjects and their endeavours. The organization built on positive energy will encourage and sustain more positive energy. Negative thoughts, deeds and processes cannot flourish or be effective amid a sea of positive thoughts, deeds and processes. The overwhelming positive energy will condemn and scatter any negativity to the far reaches of your realm.

**You are the Queen.**

**Be positive in your thoughts and actions.**

**Ultimately you are here to serve.**

**Serve your people well and they will serve you well.**

# Complementary Relationship Archetypes

As you are the Queen it is to your benefit to understand some of the archetypes that best serve your purpose. Individuals that work co-operatively and productively with you will have one or more of these archetypes. Value their service and expertise! Draw these people to you. Trust them; respect them and they will assist you in the building and maintenance of your realm.

## ∽ Servant ∾

For you as the Queen it is a great advantage to surround yourself with servants. Individuals with the Servant archetype are incredibly useful to you. They are loyal; they have remarkable organizational skills; they take care of the minor, day-to-day necessities; they are discreet; they understand never to interfere but are always willing to suggest a solution where their duty and knowledge lies; they respect each individual and the process. Without Servants you are constantly and forever working at fever pitch and within the context of minor details. With Servants you are able to devote your time and energy to more major and productive affairs.

Remember to treat your Servants with respect and dignity. When you are able, reward them for their ability and their service. Many Servants do not expect a high financial reward for their services. If you have the ability to reward them above their expectation their loyalty will stay with you. A loyal, experienced and knowledgeable servant is worth their weight in gold.

## ∽ Companion ∾

Individuals with the Companion archetype are the very best confidents. They are loyal, supportive, good listeners, non-judgmental and trustworthy. They also provide an excellent springboard for testing ideas and proposals.

There have been so many successful people who have had the support and encouragement of a Companion partner.

One famous example is Marie Curie, the dual Nobel prize-winning scientist, who had the support of her husband and fellow scientist Pierre Curie. Another example is Prince Phillip who plays the perfect companion role to Queen Elizabeth.

If you, with your Queen archetypal energy, are looking for confidants and associates to form a supportive, functioning hieratical triangle then seek the assistance of an individual with Companion archetypal energy. The Queen and the Companion have a powerful archetypal bond.

## ✥ Disciple ✥

Disciple is another archetype that blends well with the needs of the Queen energy. Individuals with the Disciple archetype are loyal, faithful and compliant. Disciples enjoy being part of a group. They love the comradeship, the social interaction, the group dynamics and the pleasure of contributing to the group's success. Disciples are willing to place the fortunes of the group ahead of their own individual desires and preferences.

Remember that you must never take these individuals for granted. These willing workers are not there for your exploitation. They are there to assist you in a helpful and dignified manner. Again, respect is the key. Take pride in the work and assistance that these individuals bring to your realm and they will reward you suitably.

## ✥ Warrior ✥

The Queen has always needed warriors. These needs are not as pressing in modern times as they were when life was more tribal and your power base relied upon the number of willing or paid conscripts you could maintain to defend your realm. However, to build a successful business, to maintain and manage a flourishing department management still relies upon the Warrior archetypal energy.

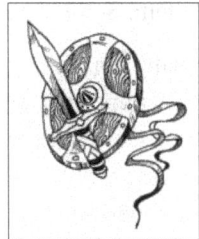

Individuals with the Warrior archetype are brave and willing to take risks. They are prepared to battle for their leader, their group and the collective cause. Like the Disciple they are willing to place aside their own individual ego and devote their time and expertise to the group. The highly social honey bee provides the perfect example of a Queen and her warriors.

# ⚜ Knight ⚜

The Knight is a special warrior. Knights have the archetypal energy of the Warrior but have a distinct place in the confidence and servitude to their Queen. Knights have a more exalted position in the hierarchy because they have proved themselves in battle and in their loyalty to their ruler.

The modern Knight is no different. These individuals with the Knight archetype are particularly daring, extremely loyal and will serve their leader to the bitter end. Knights are also charming and chivalrous. These qualities make them invaluable in business dealings with other companies.

The thing you must remember about the Knight is his love of adventure and the challenge. As the Queen, never allow the Knight to be bored or unchallenged. If this happens the Knight is likely to go off on his own adventure or cause mischief among the ranks. The key is to always give the Knight a direction and a challenge. You will be rewarded with a brave and faithful warrior.

The other aspect about the Knight that you should remember is to give them some relief and relaxation. Knights throw themselves into their work with both willingness and ferocity. They have strength, stamina and endurance that feed the belief that they can go on forever. You, the Queen, have a similar belief system. So beware of burn-out.

Finally, in days gone by, the horse, armour and weapons were the Knight's most important possessions. Today the motor car or motor bike has replaced the horse while tools have replaced the armour and weapons. Therefore tools are essential to the Knight. He should be given whatever he needs to do his job. As a mark of your respect and as a reward for his loyalty and work ethic you should also be aware of his transportation needs and desires.

# ✒ Networker ❧

In business circles the Networker is an essential and invaluable person to have. In the modern world, knowledge and communication are essential keys to business success. If you are a Queen who is involved in business, either your own individual business or as head of a department or the company, the Networker is the person that can improve your efficiency.

Networkers have the knowledge, skill and ability to find ideas, equipment or personnel that fulfils the needs of your business. The advance of technology has meant an advance in our ability to communicate more widely and rapidly than ever before. We have the ability to connect with people on the other side of the world, place and sent orders in seconds or source expertise or business needs from a vast array of resources. This specialized world of communication is the domain of the Networker. What an advantage for the Queen to attract an effective Networker or a team of Networkers into her realm. The possibilities abound and achievement multiplies when an effective team is assembled and placed into action.

# ✒ Banker ❧

Another individual useful for the Queen to bring into her realm is the person with the Banker archetype. Bankers, of course, are the best people when dealing with wealth and money. They are generally conservative and this can counter balance the influence of others within the Queen's realm, especially the Entrepreneurs. Entrepreneurs are valuable. They are fantastic with money-making ideas.

However, they are also huge risk takers and can not only make a lot of wealth but also lose a lot of wealth in a very short time. Bankers are likely to keep the spending at an affordable level. They are keen to balance the books and retain money in the coffers. Bankers can give you, the Queen, peace of mind when it comes to economic management.

# ᚖ Pioneer ᚖ

The individual with the Pioneer archetype is also a valuable person to have in your realm. These are the people that will seek new ideas, discover improved ways to do business and invent new and better business tools, systems and structures. It is like the pilgrims or explorers sending a scout ahead to check out the lay of the land, to find a safe passage and discover any dangers or pitfalls in the path ahead.

Use the Pioneer in your planning. They are the "possibility" individuals. You have the power and control to monitor their ideas. Do not be afraid to have them in your organization. Pioneers have the ability to give your realm expansion and longevity.

# ᚖ Court Jester ᚖ

The position of the Queen commands respect from her subjects. She also needs to maintain the protocols when dealing with those outside her realm. The responsibilities of the Queen are many and varied. These factors often demand that the Queen's personal interaction and communication with others is of a serious and austere nature. There also is little time for frivolity.

The best way to balance the seriousness of your role is to have a Court Jester in your employ or circle of friends. The individual with the Court Jester archetype will add lightness and humour to the occasion and the interaction. Court Jesters are brilliant at making fun of themselves and of others and doing this in a relatively non-offensive manner. Their ability to relax you and those in your company is invaluable. This allows you to assess the nature and personality of people you deal with. You can play the role of observer while your Court Jester plays the role of interaction. In days gone by the Court Jester was the spy. Through his humour he could catch the King or Queen's opponents off guard; lull them into a state of "relaxed truthfulness". Any slip in manners or protocol will be the fault of the Court Jester; not you, the Queen.

The Court Jester may, from time to time, act the fool. However, the Court Jester is no fool. Individuals with the Fool archetype are foolish and act the fool for no reason at all. Queens do not tolerate fools. Be aware of the distinction. The Court Jester is clever and witty and your ally. The Fool, especially the negative fool, is to be ignored.

## ⚜ Wise Woman ⚜

Another individual who works well with the Queen is the person who has the Sage or Wise Woman archetype. As a personal friend and companion, the Wise Woman is excellent company and a valued advisor. How do you identify a Wise Woman? Easy! They have a library full of inspirational books that delve into the practical and esoteric. If the Wise Woman cannot find what they are looking for in their library, they are happy to turn to the internet. The Queen is drawn to the Wise Woman for their knowledge and counsel. Wise Women will instinctively listen and not interfere. They will offer a range of advice and explore the possibilities. Then they leave the decision and action to you. The Wise Woman is the best life coach you will come across.

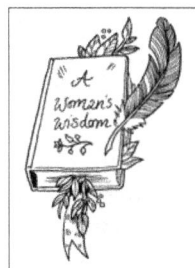

Wise Women come into their power and sphere of influence in their later years. This is usually when they have gone through much of their life doing what we all normally do. In a person's latter years there is more time or a conscious decision made to devote to the Wise Woman aspects of their personality. However, the Wise Woman has the same nature and ability all her life. This means that there are young people who have the Wise Woman archetype. They are not to be ignored because of their age. Wisdom is wisdom, irrespective of time and age.

## ⚜ King ⚜

The King and the Queen working together is a powerful force. If you have a King in your life, your reign as the Queen will be enhanced enormously if you remember the definitive golden rule.

**Define your territory.**

**Never encroach on the King's territory and insist that he not encroach on yours.**

Communication is so important between Kings and Queens. While others in your realm will follow your commands and do your bidding the King will not. You therefore need to establish where the responsibilities lie.

- ❖ What falls within your domain?
- ❖ What falls within the King's domain?
- ❖ What responsibilities can be shared.

When this is established and put into practice, harmony exists and progress moves at a great pace. The strong energetic drive of a King and a Queen working in harmony is a powerful force. All things may be achieved and at a rapid rate. The realm will expand with purpose and cohesion. There will be a strong bond of loyalty between the Queen and her subjects when they see the strong bond of loyalty between the Queen and the King.

## ❧ Avenger ☙

The administration of rules and justice is the guiding energy of the Avenger. Remember that all archetypes have both positive and negative energy. For many people, the word Avenger may conjure up thoughts of revenge, retaliation and brutality. We see examples of this behaviour and the employment of these negative personality traits on a daily basis. However, the positive Avenger archetypal energy is about guidance, personal adherence to the rules and demanding justice for all. The positive Avenger is about strength of character rather than physical strength or enforcement.

When the Queen associates with a positive Avenger the rules and sense of justice is reinforced. When the Queen acts with positive energy and this message is amplified by the positive Avenger all those within the realm are reassured of their safety and worthiness. They are doubly protected.

The Avenger may also act as a safety mechanism for the Queen. When tough decisions need to be made the Avenger is there, not only to protect the Queen but also to reinforce those decisions. When the rules apply and justice is not only done but seen to be done then tough decisions can be made with positive acknowledge. This process will lead to a continuation of peace and stability.

# Employment ~ Vocation

## Business Management

Queens are born to rule, take control and manage. There are successful Queens in all levels of management. If you are part of a company or if you manage your own business, you are there partly because of your Queen archetype. It is that part of your personality that gives you the skills and characteristics necessary for the position.

Your business success will expand if you have a working knowledge of those nine aspects that make up the archetypal energy of the Queen.

A reminder; they are respect, understanding your realm, planning, affirmation, delegation, being proud, striving for longevity, looking after the royal coffers and being a Queen of service.

**Stay positive in these aspects and the achievements will fall into place.**

Also remember the more quality people you bring to support you and your business endeavours, the more your business will expand and succeed. Examine the people that surround you. Are they suitable? Do they have the necessary archetypal energy that supports you or hinders you? Do you praise their positive qualities or become frustrated with their negative qualities? You are the Queen. You are in charge and in control. Your action, more than anything else, determines results.

## Education and Teaching

If you have the Queen archetype and are in education you are in a suitable profession. Do not be concerned how far up the hierarchical chain you are. You may be a classroom teacher, the head of your department, the school principal or Vice-Chancellor of the university. They are all suitable positions. You have established your realm. You have your subjects. There are established protocols within your organization. There are other protocols that you have established.

You have dealings with other realms. You are using your Queen archetype for your personal development and in the service that will benefit many others.

Remember that you are in an entrusted position. You are dealing with the minds, opinions and personalities of others. The key is respect. As a Queen you will have to deal with individuals that have archetypes and archetypal energy that will test your metal. Queens do not tolerate Fools. Individuals with the Fool archetype still need education. Queens find Damsels and Princesses difficult to deal with. Damsels are in love with love; often waiting for their Knight to rescue them and have a self-esteem that goes from high to low at a regular and rapid rate. The Queen cannot afford such self-indulgence and needs all her tolerance to deal successfully with these individuals. So too, the Princess; whose station is below that of the Queen; whose desire for comfort and security of the home or castle paramount; whose willingness to shop and spend is remarkable and whose love of trivialities is a total source of frustration. These individuals will test your resolve but they will still be part of your realm and your duty is to serve them and bring out their best.

You may be the Queen. You may be in charge. However, you are still there to serve and educate.

## ⚜ Government ❧

All levels of government also have suitable positions for those with the Queen archetype. From Prime Minister down to Mayor or department head you will find individuals with the Queen archetype.

The key to success and longevity is to remember that you are in the service industry. This is not easy for a King or Queen to remember. There are so many responsibilities; so many people and issues to deal with; so many staff that are below you and that are seen as servants it is easy to lose focus on the service ideal. How often do you hear politicians say that they got into politics to make a difference; to be altruistic; to help others? How often do they fall into the trap of partisanship, paternalism; self-importance and the quest for power and control?

**The Queen is there to serve.**

# ⊰ Motherhood and Family ⊱

Mothers can also have the Queen archetype. This does not diminish your power as a Queen. On the contrary you have chosen a vocation that is fundamental in determining the type of society you aspire to. Your family values; your modelling of behaviour for your children; the decisions you must make for them when they are unable to make them for themselves; the way you and your family interact with your neighbours and your community; all add to the society in which you live.

Never undervalue your role as a mother or the head of a household. You have chosen a fundamental service role. The existence and strength of society depend upon this service.

# Summary

**Treasure yourself and your attributes.**

**It is a wonderful gift to have a Queen archetype.**

You have those leadership qualities to take control and be in charge; you are able to watch your realm grow and flourish; you have the opportunity to provide a rich tapestry of tradition and pageantry; you have the ability to encourage, stimulate and provide the opportunity for those within your realm to grow, fulfil their potential and be a part of a communal, successful venture; you can establish a model realm that can be an inspiration to other individuals and other realms.

As with all leadership there is also hard work and responsibilities. As a Queen you are always capable of rising to the occasion. You have the qualities of personal strength, courage, endurance and resilience. Make the most of them and lead from the front. Stay true to your Queen archetype and she will serve you well. Who knows what realm you may create? Only you and the future will determine what you can achieve and what influence you may have?

## Remember!

## Rule with authority and benevolence

## Achieve your ambitions and goals

## Be loved and admired by your subjects and all those who surround you.

# Your Royal Photograph

# Plans to expand your Realm

# About the Author

Brian Dale is as an archetype consultant, past life hypnotherapist and workshop facilitator. He is a retired primary school teacher, librarian and storyteller.

Brian's giftedness in archetypes was an amazing discovery. In 2002, he trained as an archetype consultant at the Australian Institute of Caroline Myss. Archetypes are universal personifications, such as, Princess, King, Victim, Warrior, Rescuer and many more. We continually use archetypal energy in our daily lives. Brian realized he could assist people in the discovery and understanding of their true selves, how they operate in the various aspects of their lives and how to bring change for their betterment and the betterment of others.

*Archetypes give us an understanding of who we truly are. They are an incredible tool for self-empowerment. They allow us to change our lives when we move from the negative aspect of an archetype to the positive aspect of that archetype.*

Brian's intuition and insightful observations have assisted many people to fully understand, empower and change themselves and their situation. He has given talks and lectures and facilitated archetype workshops throughout Australia.

Recently, with the passing of his daughter, Tahla, Brian has been inspired to investigate the Afterlife. This has taken him on a new and exciting pathway. He has had several experiences as a medium. He was also encouraged to train as a QHHT practitioner. This is Delores Cannon's past life hypnotherapy technique.

*"This is a new and stimulating journey. As a medium and hypnotherapist I am relishing each and every experience."*

Brian is a published author and his stories for children have been used in standardized tests by both the Victorian and South Australian Education Departments. One of his greatest passions is drama and the performing arts. Brian is owner and teacher of Byron/Ballina Bright Lights Performance School.

Brian and his wife Robyn have been married for over forty years, have three wonderful children, Adam, Jade and Tahla and the most amazing grandchildren, Luca, Lilly and Isla.

# Other Books by the Author

*Archetypes, unmasking your true self* (Possumwood, 2012)
*Tilly and the Magic Potion* (Possumwood, 2013)
*Self-Esteem Matters* (Possumwood, 2015)
*Decoding the Afterlife* (Possumwood 2016)
*The Knight* (Possumwood 2017)

# Contact the Author

*Email: briandale1@bigpond.com*
*Web: briandale.com.au*
    *possumwoodpublishing.com*